Goodbyes I Never told

AF624603

Lincy Panicker

BookLeaf Publishing

Presentation by *BookLeaf Publishing*

Web: www.bookleafpub.com

E-mail: info@bookleafpub.com

ISBN: 9789357215756

First edition 2022

10-01-17

Thank you for everything.

The good and the bad.

The joy and the lessons.

I will never not wish you everything under the sun and then some.

Goodbye.

ACKNOWLEDGEMENT

To those who collected the last mangled brittle bones of my sanity, pieced it together, validated my pain, and reminded me how much more I was than where I found myself. To those who reminded me that love isn't holding onto mere morsels of faulty inconsistent communication that left me in constant limbo with self created idealization to compensate for what has stopped being there for quite some time.

PREFACE

Here is to the raw art that can only be born in the lowest low. Here is to boundaries and healing. Here is to the strength of the vulnerability of your soft heart to still believe. Here is to saying goodbyes to the past in order to say hello to the future. Here is to demanding better for yourself. Here is to trusting the intuitions of your decisions and never again second guessing them. Here is to truly letting go of the sweetest things that you were certain would never turn sour. They no longer serve your today.

Hope was never meant to make you shed tears for years and leave you confused. Love was never meant to keep you questioning why you weren't worth the bare minimum.

Say Your Peace. Then Let Go.

The 2x Equation:

They never told me about the equation:
"For every great love
your heart will break twice."

Once when he holds your hand for the last time,
Once again when he holds her hand for the first time.

Once when the sparkle in his eyes when he looks at you disappears,
Once again when the sparkle reappears in his eyes besmirched by her.

Once when he closes the chapter with you,
Once again when he begins a chapter anew

Once when you realize you're not the one he marries,
Once again when it's someone new his heart carries.

Once when you still hide away trinkets of memories tethered to foolish hope.
Once again when you've finally accepted that you stand alone at the end of the rope.

Here's to everything we almost were,
And here's to everything we will become,

Individually,
in spite of what we almost were.

Yes, I walked away
but I just now realized,
I never truly learned to let you go,
all the way from here.

Once was enough

Loving you was enough to know
that I never want to love another person the way I loved you.
Loving you was the first time
I thought I could lose someone I would fall apart without.

Loving you was easy,
like Arabian sands effortlessly filling the cracks
amidst jagged rocks
in a curious toddler's beach jar.

Loving you was my bones being churned into sawdust.
Yet infatuation numbed to it,
I saw only the spit out remains in the wind
that glistened like pixie dust.

Loving you was an anvil
that I carried in my fondest memories
adorned in the finest gold,
held on a granite pedestal
that perched upon my aorta.

Loving you was needing to make you smile
even if it meant making myself fold like origami,
just to make you stay a while.

Loving you was "I thought I figured out the directions to your love
only to find out you reoriented the entire geography of your soul."

Loving you was "I would saw my right arm off for you,
but I cannot in good conscience bring children into the world with you."

Loving you was both heavy and too special and the last thing I ever felt great at.
Loving you was easy

until you weren't you anymore.

Pangea

Pangea envied you and I you know.
Intertwined like hand-kneaded dough,
Our demarcations were long buried under our joy,
Unconcerned with trivial matters of man,
like where you ended and where I began.

You couldn't tell me
I wasn't built of the same mold that created you,
because we made sense
in all the ways one soul does.

So, when we evolved and shifted,
When millimeter by millimeter we drifted,
When tectonic plates under our feet lifted,
faintly, like a dying man's pulse undetected,

We didn't even notice.

Now you are a speck from my finest telescope,
As I search for what we once were at the highest magnification.

And it has become truly impossible,
To still gaslight the existence of the ocean
that roars ferociously between us.

Flameless

I always get burned
by the candles
that were never lit for me

By those for whom
I would I torch whole villages for

How do I learn to love
Less?

My "This is Why" Chapter

I will forevermore point to you
and call you:
My "This is why" Chapter.

This is why being loved
makes me nauseous.
This is why being cherished
leaves me callused.
This is why being held
makes me stiff.
This is why I'll always wonder
what if

I hadn't walked away.

I Promise You

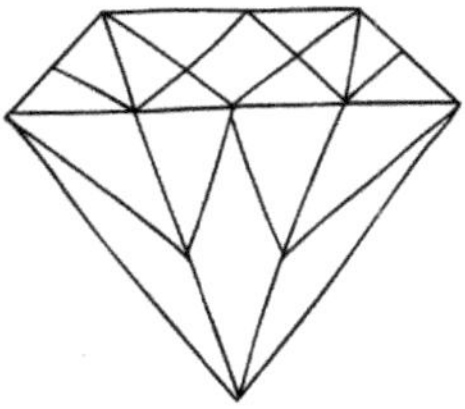

There is something you should know:
The hardest thing I've ever done
Is let you go.

I let you go
because I saw it before you did.
I saw the ugly truth rear its head:
That it was never due to a lack of love,
but that we were on journeys
that pointed to opposite ends.

Oh, what I would have done
to hold your hand until the very end.

You see,
in choosing you,
I would have lost me.
And in letting you choose me,
you would have lost you.

And I could never do that to you.

But I promise you,
I searched.
I searched high and low in the darkest valleys
to find a loophole in fate where it would end with you.

I promise you,
If there was a Morse code scraped together in the depths
of an ancient cave that held the solution
I would have given my life for it.

I promise you,
I would have moved mountains
To make you and I work.
If there was even an inkling of possibility of a future
that we would survive it,
I would have found it.

We were worth that much.

But you were worth more.

Freezing Nostalgia

I walked away
even though it just about killed me.
Because on our last days I often felt alone
when I was in your company.

But the only thing that made me feel alive
was recounting all the ways you and I,
were still you and I.

When you were no longer around to say goodnight,
I played it back from memories of past nights
on a loop,
A vintage record player I hid in my attic was all I could recoup.

Because you had become someone I no longer recognized.

So I soothed my soul on restless nights
with trinkets of who you once were.

I swear I tried.
I tried when I dressed my emptiness with fleeting moments.
I tried when I contoured my pain.
I tried when I decided to leave you in the shadows.
I tried when I attempted to lose you in the arms of another.
I tried.

Because no matter how much
I wanted our last pages to be one and the same,
you and I would never work.

Yet I kept finding myself mesmerized by the rear view.

I tried to stop loving you.

I really did believe 2 years was enough time
for my heart to catch up to my brain.

Vintage Price Tag

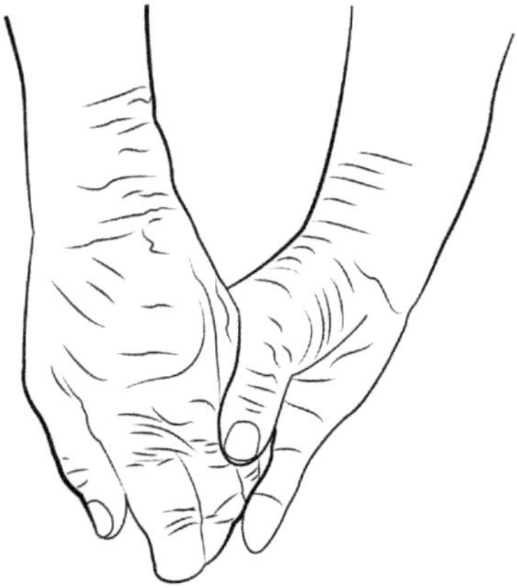

It never had much back support.
It felt made of cheap cloth and plywood.
It was hardly ever aesthetically pleasing.
We often lost more than remotes in its corners.

But we fell in love on that grey couch you know.
Over a box of pizza and 40 hours of conversation.
Spoke so long that we missed the fair.
And how I laughed in your face
When you said we would go next year.

I laughed at how on the first date,
You knew you would still be here next year.

And how I hate to say you were right.

So, we went the next year,
And the year after that,
And the year after that.
We got our faces painted to last
Caricatures that couldn't hope to measure up to our joy at that.

But this year you hold her hand.

Does she know the way we laughed and laughed?

How we found ourselves in each other's missing parts?
Does she know the history of that couch
with its paw prints and jagged marks?

Now you want to sell it.
For a profit.
But I need to know:

Did you add the value of our memories?
The worth of the beginning of our love story?

Unequivocal

You absolutely can do
anything you want
to do.

It's just that you did
what I would never
do to you.

Apologies

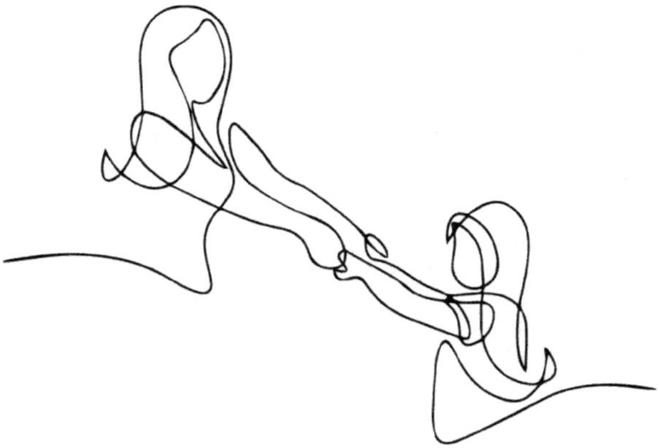

Dear Me,
I am sorry that you still hear ringing in your ears
From bombs that dropped in your early years.

I am sorry you still side-step on clean floors
afraid of the glass shards that once pierced your core.

I am sorry that you still hear the shattering
of the moment it dawned on you,
that you never meant to them what they did you.

I am sorry you still hear the deafening silence,
of the aftershock of the unspeakable violence
that made you find refuge in lone islands.

I am sorry
that every time you feel slighted
intentional or not,
you get ignited,
as betrayal echoes through dormant chambers
that once again steal your slumber,
triggering revolting lava that makes you burn,
that makes you terrified to know which way to turn
that awaken sleeping monsters of your past
that claw its way out to your present.

I am sorry you always get caught in crossfires
that haven't been fired
outside the realms of your twisted mind.

I'm sorry that you're certain the asphalt will shift,
that the grounds of the earth will rift,
and swallow you hole into a wormhole
to the moment he stole the innocence of your soul.

Perhaps someday,

you won't gasp for air
with punctured lungs laid on ocean floors bare

As you stand on concrete.

Summer

They assure me sunshine will come
once again.
They swear by it you know.

So here I am,
awaiting the warmth
I've only ever known from you.

I might be insane,
because there is no more you
and somehow there should be sunshine.
And I can't comprehend how the two
can exist without the other.

I'm crazy if I don't believe them
because I know the truth
of your presence.

I'm crazy if I do believe them
because they tell me of hope.

But I know better.

Folded Corners

If I'm being honest,
I said I finished the chapter of you and I,
and I did.

At least I said I did.
I never meant to lie.
I swear I tried to flip the page and read on,
To move on.

But between you and I,
I left the corners of your pages folded over,
so I can revisit them over and over
in all the days I needed the warmth of your cover.

When no one was looking over my shoulder,
I read the page where you
turn the heat on,

when I step out of the shower wet,
when I get in the car on a cold day,
when I sleep at night in your arms.

Apparently
I've only ever associated warmth with you,

And now I'm in a blizzard alone.

Veteran on the Run

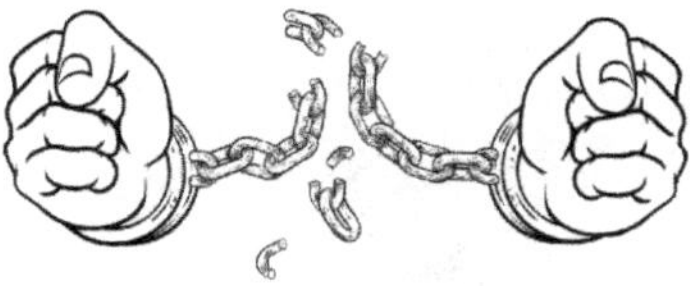

I feel fraudulent,
every time someone calls me resilient.
You see Purple Hearts aren't earned
by those who took side routes to avoid burns.

I never let myself get submerged in reality
I took shield in the shallow attention,
of faceless persons constantly.
I outran the crippling brokenness of yesterday.
Self-assured it wouldn't catch me on the run
if I disguised myself in sparkling moments of disarray
if I convinced myself I could just not serve my time,

eventually it would lose steam and give up
and stop hunting me at least in this lifetime.

Perhaps there is nothing honorary
about prolonging the near death grip of pain.
because it still found a way to catch up to me.

I didn't know then,
of the sweet release
in claiming my purple heart,
in letting my tired feet rest at last.

Perhaps after this sentence to feel and truly heal,
I could remember to live
And not merely just survive.

Subjective Muse

I tattooed the magic of you into my veins
and grafted you into the grey matter of my brain.

Then without warning you shape-shifted,
until that version of you no longer existed,
except the parts engrained into my very being.

It only pains me
that I can’t ever point out my original muse
to those who insist such beauty
can never exist in ways
that can be realistically manifested.

I used to think they were nay sayers,
Unbelievers.

Now I know it was always me
who was crazy
enough to believe
you were who you pretended to be.

How it stings to know my truth was just your make believe.

Army of One

Dear sweet soul:

You're not the problem
You're not crazy
You're not overreacting
And You're not confrontational

For standing up for you
when they took a seat.
For having your own back
when they turned theirs on you.
For demanding your voice to be heard
when they expected you just be part of the herd.
For expressing your hurt
when they minimized the source of your pain.
For walking away when you deserved the truth
from those who sat silently.

You see when those who say “I’m here for You”
are the same ones
who saw the dagger sharpened for You,
and had the power to warn you,
and just chose to be bystanders,

those words sting of gangrenous infection
ripping new layers
in twice ripped open wounds of your soul.

The most cruel thing a person can do,
is to call you family
and not mean it
when you most needed them to be.

Do You Remember?

Do you remember how afraid I was to say I love you back?
Do you remember how I curled my tongue inward and swallowed it in me and shushed it away into deep lullabies but how it still grew wings inside of me until it could no longer be contained?
Do you remember the first time It fell out of my mouth like it took on a life of its own?
Do you remember how I was physically unable to stop saying it?

And that's when you decided you were able to stop

But you kept saying it anyway
long after I walked away.
Making me believe I should find a way.
Time and time again to hold on to our yesterday.

Do you know how much more it hurts that you hung onto me
Until the moment you jumped ship overnight into your next story?
And still leaned on me for security simultaneously?

Stepping Stone

I thought I infected you.
So I sucked the venom out of you
that no one knew about.

I emptied the joy of my soul
into a barren well hushing my own voice
to make space for your poison.
Slurping up the way your words hurt me
hoping it would be enough
for you to come back to you.

Even if not for me.

I put a central IV in your veins
And connected it to my soul
And pulled in all your rage
And I took it all in,
Hoping the man I once knew
would come alive again.

How I bit down on my lips
because it hurt every time you lashed out.
Every time you got loud
when often all I did
was ask if your body was hurting you
So I could find ways to heal you.

You breathed again.

But you came back
With green skin
and nuts and bolts
of shoddy craftsmanship.
With jagged lips
Sewn carelessly together
by a child lacking dexterity.
Formed of ugly unfamiliar pieces
I no longer recognized

And then you used what was left of my body of sacrifice
as a stepping stone into your new life.

And your parting words
were that this was God's will.

Impeccable

It was always me.

I was the magic
That made you look like a spell.

It was the pedestal I built you
that made you seem so infallible.

It was my butterflies
that made you taste like freedom.

It was my rainbow
That made you seem so extraordinarily vibrant.

It was my finite pixie dust particles
That made you glisten.

It was my rose-colored vision
That made you look like a dream

It was my flame
that illuminated you,
that caught a light just right
That made you look so impeccable

The way you move now,
You have never seemed so painfully average.

Home

When we ended,
I kept welcoming you into the only place
That was home to me.

The only place I've ever felt safe or seen.
The only place I let my bare feet finally touch the floor.
The only place I hung my woes.
The only place I could unload my pain.
While I set a plate for you at my table,
you pulled out the seat from beneath me.
You poured gasoline on the softest ground I have ever known
and handed them all lit matches
and told me I could still call this home.

While I set a plate for you at my table,
you pulled out the chair beneath me.

In this home that you are only in
Because I kept opening the door for you.
Then you turned it into my personal gas chamber
And said "I never told you to leave"

And you used that as a stepping stone
Into your next life.

I told you how it hurt me
How seeing your face hurts me
How I needed space to heal from you.
How I needed to feel like I had a home without you.

And you apologized
And then you showed up again
two days later-
When my wounds were still
this fresh.

Merry Christmas

My Black Dress

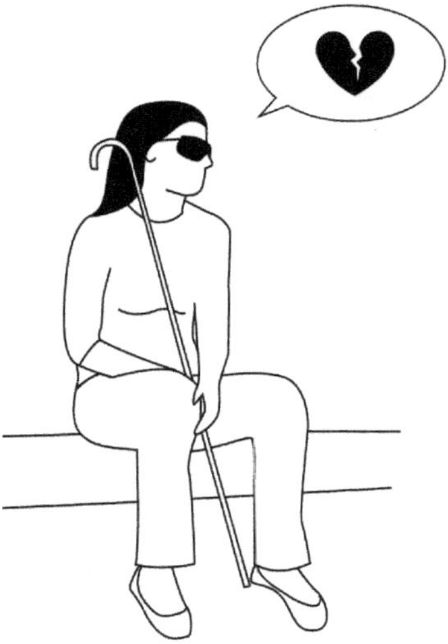

You were in a comatose state
And I toiled over your dead weight
With bated breath I waited
For a sign of life
That you were coming back

Even if not for me

Once in a blue moon
You wiggled the tip of your fingers
In a way that was a fraction of familiar
And into that I overflowed my cup of hope
Nestled in certainty that you'd come back to you

Even if not for me.

And then I waited some more

For another sign,

for the next morsel of hope I could cradle into tomorrow.

Apparently you have been gone
and everyone attended your funeral
While I alone waited for another sign of life

Apparently I have been sitting in your shed dead skin
trying to breathe life into you with our fondest memories
so assured that if I try hard enough you will be you again.

Apparently it was always just rigor mortis
that somehow lasted 2 years.

Today I put on my black dress,
with your eulogy tucked into my pocket.

Scattered Scraps: A Collection of Intrusive Thoughts that never found its home

We have endless hours to recount
what went wrong.
But what went right
Felt just like magic.

You and I were nothing short of magic
Yet it seems I alone stand disillusioned

I lit up every time you were even in my vicinity.
So I was blindsided that you were the one
who put out my light for what seems a dark eternity.

Perhaps if I found myself first,
I wouldn't have so desperately
searched for myself
in you.

Here's to all the times
I swallowed my truth
to keep you
from raising your voice.

I've never been sure of anything.
I've never been sure of myself
or the length of time
those around me would last.
The only thing I have ever been sure of
Was your kindness and compassion.

And if that was a lie
I am not sure if I've ever known
Any truth

Jekyll and Hyde

It will never make sense to me,
how the most intimate sunshine I've ever known
and the most vicious hailstorm I've ever endured,
rained down from the same soul.

She said you are so lucky.
"If you feel pain like this
You experience the full spectrum of life
So imagine your joy.

I didn't know how to say
I would rather be numb than happy.
If this is the coldness that awaited me on the other side.

Your kindness vanished
And I am here
Grasping at smoke and mirrors
At holograms
Wasted energy

I mourned us because you're the only one I ever wrote vows for
I reread them lately
they were always meant for you
when you used to be you

I think the day I cried more because of who you are
than the days I laughed with who you were
Was the nail in the coffin
That my weak hands were too foolishly hopeful to push all the way in

---

Because you dealt in legal ramifications
While I dealt in pure consideration to the human soul

If time was a measure of healing,
perhaps it wouldn't feel like we parted
Yesterday

And maybe someday,
I'll stop breaking my own heart
for the way I broke you.

If you were to grind my entire being into the finest of powders,
you still wouldn't find a quarter ounce of me that hates you,
and that's truly why I hate you

Because I wish I could.

The Burning Woman Festival

I feel like I'm constantly on fire.
Truly ablaze.
The marrow of my bones burning.
My nerve endings screaming,
but somehow not dying.
Every ounce of my being
seeking asylum from me.

You all walk past me on the street
It's just another Tuesday.

And to get to you
To get to the core of you
To get your love from you
You wanted me to morphe into you
Until I was

no longer me

What hurts the most
Is that I wouldn't have changed
a thing about you,
while I made excuses
for the way you spoke to me
like you never would anyone else.

www.ingramcontent.com/pod-product-compliance
Lightning Source LLC
Chambersburg PA
CBHW051744130826
49812CB00033B/994
* 9 7 8 9 3 5 7 2 1 5 7 5 6 *